American History Series
Interactive Notebook: Reconstruction
Grades 5–8

Author: Schyrlet Cameron

Editor: Mary Dieterich

Proofreaders: Alexis Fey and Margaret Brown

COPYRIGHT © 2022 Mark Twain Media, Inc.

ISBN 978-1-62223-861-3

Printing No. CD-405069

Mark Twain Media, Inc., Publishers
Distributed by Carson Dellosa Education

Table of Contents

Introduction

Interactive Notebook: Reconstruction is one of several books in Mark Twain Media's new American History Series of interactive notebooks. This series provides students in grades 5 through 8 with opportunities to explore the significant events and people that make up American history.

Creating and Using an Interactive Notebook

Interactive Notebook: Reconstruction is designed to allow students to become active participants in their own learning. The book lays out an easy-to-follow plan for setting up, creating, and maintaining the interactive notebook. Once completed, the notebook becomes a great resource for reviewing and studying for tests.

How the Book Is Organized

The 19 lessons contained in Interactive Notebook: Reconstruction cover four units of study: Lincoln Begins Second Term as President, President Andrew Johnson and Restoration, Reconstruction and President Ulysses S. Grant, and End of Reconstruction. The units can be used in the order presented or in an order that best fits the classroom or home school curriculum. Teachers can easily differentiate units to address the individual learning levels and needs of students. The lessons are designed to support state and national standards. Each lesson consists of three pages. Teachers need to make the necessary number of copies of the Student Instructions, Key Details, and Left-hand Pages for each student to use. Students then use those pages to create the left- and right-hand pages of their interactive notebooks.

- **Right-hand page:** essential information for understanding the lesson concepts. Answers to the Demonstrate and Reflect activities can be written on this page, or an additional page may need to be added for those answers.
- **Left-hand page:** hands-on activity such as a foldable or graphic organizer to help students process essential information from the lesson.

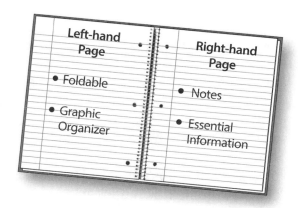

Organizing an Interactive Notebook

What Is an Interactive Notebook?

Does this sound familiar? "I can't find my homework…class notes…study guide." If so, the interactive notebook is a tool students can use to help manage this problem. An interactive notebook is simply a notebook that students use to record, store, and organize their work. The "interactive" aspect of the notebook comes from the fact that students are working with information in various ways as they fill in the notebook. Once completed, the notebook becomes the student's own personalized study guide and a great resource for reviewing information, reinforcing concepts, and studying for tests.

Materials Needed to Create an Interactive Notebook

- Notebook (spiral, composition, or binder with loose-leaf paper)
- Glue stick
- Scissors

- Colored pencils (we do not recommend using markers)
- Tabs

Creating an Interactive Notebook

A good time to introduce the interactive notebook is at the beginning of a new unit of study. Use the following steps to get started.

Step 1: *Notebook Cover*

Students design a cover to reflect the units of study. They should add their name and other important information as directed by the teacher.

Step 2: *Grading Rubric*

Take time to discuss the grading rubric with the students. It is important for each student to understand the expectations for creating the interactive notebook.

Step 3: *Table of Contents*

Students label the first several pages of the notebook "Table of Contents." When completing a new page, they then add its title to the table of contents.

Step 4: *Creating Pages*

The notebook is developed using the dual-page format. The right-hand side is the input page where essential information, Demonstrate and Reflect answers, and notes from readings, lectures, or videos are placed. The left-hand side is the output page reserved for folding activities, charts, graphic organizers, etc. Students number the front and back of each page in the bottom outside corner (odd: LEFT-side; even: RIGHT-side).

Step 5: *Tab Units*

Add a tab to the edge of the first page of each unit to make it easy to flip to the unit.

Step 6: *Glossary*

Students reserve several pages at the back of the notebook where they can create a glossary of domain-specific terms encountered in each lesson.

Step 7: *Pocket*

Students should attach a pocket to the inside of the back cover of the notebook for storage of handouts, returned quizzes, class syllabus, and other items that don't seem to belong on pages of the notebook. This can be an envelope, resealable plastic bag, or students can design their own pocket.

Left-hand and Right-hand Notebook Pages

Interactive notebooks are usually viewed open like a textbook. This allows the student to view the left-hand page and right-hand page at the same time. You have several options for how to format the two pages. Traditionally, the right-hand page is used as the input or the content part of the lesson. The left-hand page is the student output part of the lesson. This is where the students have an opportunity to show what they have learned in a creative and colorful way. (Color helps the brain remember information better.) The note-book image on the right details different types of items and activities that could be included for each page.

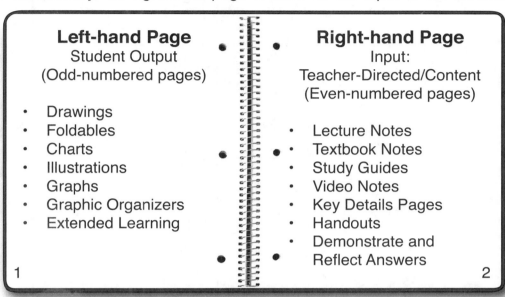

The format of the interactive notebook involves both the right-brain and left-brain hemispheres to help students process information. When creating the pages, start with the left-hand page. First, have students date the page. Students then move to the right-hand page and the teacher-directed part of the lesson. Finally, students use the information they have learned to complete the left-hand page. Below is an example of completed right- and left-hand pages.

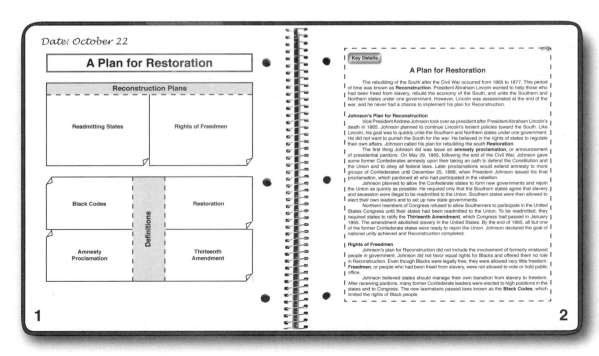

Interactive Notebook Grading Rubric

Directions: Review the criteria for the grading rubric that will be used to score your completed notebook. Place this page in your notebook.

Reconstruction Interactive Notebook Grading Rubric

Category	Excellent (4)	Good Work (3)	Needs Improvement (2)	Incomplete (1)	
Table of Contents	Table of contents is complete.	Table of contents is mostly complete.	Table of contents is somewhat incomplete.	Attempt was made to include table of contents.	
Organization	All notebook pages are in correct order. All are numbered, dated, and titled correctly.	Most pages are in correct order. Most are numbered, dated, and titled correctly.	Some pages are in correct order. Some are numbered, dated, and titled correctly.	Few pages are in correct order. Few are numbered, dated, and titled correctly.	
Content	All information complete, accurate, and placed in the correct order. All spelling correct.	Most information complete, accurate, and placed in the correct order. Most spelling correct.	Some information complete, accurate, and placed in the correct order. Some spelling errors.	Few pages correctly completed. Many spelling errors.	
Appearance	All notebook pages are neat and colorful.	Most notebook pages are neat and colorful.	Some notebook pages are neat and colorful.	Few notebook pages are neat and colorful.	

Teacher's Comments:

Reconstruction Era Timeline

1863 **Dec. 8:** President Lincoln issued the Proclamation of Amnesty and Reconstruction

1865 **Mar. 3:** Congress established the Freedmen's Bureau.
Mar. 4: President Lincoln began his second term as president.
Apr. 9: The Civil War effectively ended when General Robert E. Lee and Confederate troops surrendered at Appomattox Court House, Virginia.
Apr. 14: President Lincoln was assassinated by John Wilkes Booth.
Apr. 15: Andrew Johnson became the 17th president.
Dec. 18: The Thirteenth Amendment abolished slavery.

1866 **Feb. 19:** The new Freedmen's Bureau bill was passed.
Apr. 9: The Civil Rights Act was passed.

1867 **Mar. 2:** The first Reconstruction Act was passed.
Mar. 2: The Tenure of Office Act was passed.
Mar. 23: The second Reconstruction Act was passed.
Jul. 8: The third Reconstruction Act was passed.

1868 **Feb. 24:** Congress voted to Impeach President Andrew Johnson.
Feb. 27: The fourth Reconstruction Act was passed.
Mar. 23: President Andrew Johnson's impeachment trial began.
May 16: President Johnson was acquitted.
Jul. 28: The Fourteenth Amendment was passed.
Nov. 3: Ulysses S. Grant was elected president.
Dec. 25: Unconditional amnesty was granted to all participants in the "insurrection or rebellion" against the United States.

1870 **Feb. 25:** Hiram Revels of Mississippi became the first African-American senator.
Mar. 30: The Fifteenth Amendment was adopted.
Jun. 27: Congress established the Department of Justice.
Jul. 14: The Naturalization Act was passed.

1871 **Feb. 28:** The Federal Election Law was passed.

1872 **Nov. 5:** President Ulysses S. Grant was reelected.

1875 **Mar. 1:** The Civil Rights Act was passed.

1876 **Dec. 6:** Rutherford B. Hayes was elected president, ending Reconstruction.

5

Student Instructions: Lincoln and Slavery

Materials Needed

Glue, scissors, colored pencils

How to Create a Right-hand Interactive Notebook Page

Read the Key Details page. Then cut out the page and attach it to the right-hand page of your interactive notebook. Use what you have learned to create the left-hand page.

How to Create a Left-hand Interactive Notebook Page

Complete the following steps to create the left-hand page of your interactive notebook. Use lots of color.

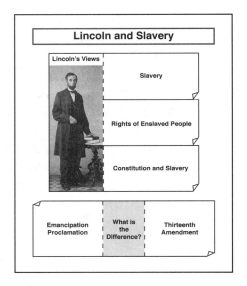

Step 1: Cut out the title and glue it to the top of the notebook page.

Step 2: Cut out *Lincoln's Views* flap book. Cut on the solid lines to create three flaps. Apply glue to the back of the picture section and attach it below the title. Under each flap, summarize Lincoln's views.

Step 3: Cut out the *What is the Difference?* flap book. Apply glue to the gray center section and attach it at the bottom of the page. Under each flap, write the definition.

Demonstrate and Reflect on What You Have Learned

Read the words of Abraham Lincoln below. Think about what you learned from the reading selection. In your interactive notebook, write your opinion of what Lincoln said. Explain what you think he meant. Support your opinion with specific details or examples.

> *"Let us discard all this quibbling about this man and that man—this race and the other race, being inferior, and therefore they must be placed in an inferior position. Let us discard all these things, and unite as one people throughout the land, until we shall once more stand up declaring that all men are created equal."*

Key Details

Lincoln and Slavery

Abraham Lincoln served as the sixteenth president from 1861 to 1865. The Civil War ended in 1865. Lincoln's views on slavery evolved over the years, and he was able to bring about social and political change during his time in office.

Lincoln's Views on Slavery

Lincoln was opposed to slavery. He and his family never owned slaves. He once said, "As I would not be a slave, so I would not be a master. This expresses my idea of democracy." He argued that the phrase "All men are created equal" from the Declaration of Independence applied to Black people and white people alike. However, he did not believe Blacks and whites should have the same rights. In 1858, during his race for the U.S. Senate with Stephen Douglas, Lincoln stated: "I will say then that I am not, nor ever have been, in favor of bringing about in any way the social and political equality of the white and black races, that I am not nor ever have been in favor of making voters or jurors of negroes, nor of qualifying them to hold office, nor to intermarry with white people;…"

The United States Constitution did not mention the word *slavery*, but there were clauses protecting it. Lincoln believed "the Congress of the United States has no power, under the Constitution, to interfere with the institution of slavery..." where it already existed.

Lincoln opposed the expansion of slavery. He stated his views during his first presidential campaign. "I will not abolish slavery where it already exists, but we must not let the practice spread. I am opposed to allowing slavery in the new territories."

Emancipation Proclamation

When Abraham Lincoln issued the **Emancipation Proclamation** on January 1, 1863, he freed enslaved people in all states or parts of states in rebellion against the United States—about one million people. However, this did not include freedom for the three million enslaved people in states that had not seceded from the Union or even in certain areas of states that had seceded. The states that had formed the Confederacy ignored the order. Millions of people remained enslaved.

Soldier reading the Emancipation Proclamation to enslaved people

Thirteenth Amendment

Lincoln pushed Congress to make slavery illegal. On December 18, 1865, the **Thirteenth Amendment** to the Constitution of the United States finally freed all enslaved people within the United States and made slavery illegal forever. It also gave Congress the power to enforce this amendment. However, the formerly enslaved people were not considered citizens and did not have the right to vote.

Southern Blacks now faced the difficulty Northern Blacks had confronted—that of freedmen surrounded by hostile white people. One **freedman**, or formerly enslaved man, Houston Hartsfield Holloway, wrote, "For we colored people did not know how to be free, and the white people did not know how to have a free colored person about them."

Lincoln and Slavery

Lincoln's Views	
	**Slavery**
	Rights of Enslaved People
	Constitution and Slavery

Emancipation Proclamation	**What is the Difference?**	**Thirteenth Amendment**

Student Instructions: Reconstruction and President Lincoln

Materials Needed

Glue, scissors, colored pencils

How to Create a Right-hand Interactive Notebook Page

Read the Key Details page. Then cut out the box and attach it to the right-hand page of your interactive notebook. Use what you have learned to create the left-hand page.

How to Create a Left-hand Interactive Notebook Page

Complete the following steps to create the left-hand page of your interactive notebook. Use lots of color.

Step 1: Cut out the title and glue it to the top of the notebook page.

Step 2: Cut out the *Reconstruction of the South* flap piece. Apply glue to the gray tab and attach it below the title. Under the flap, briefly explain the reason for rebuilding the Southern states after the Civil War.

Step 3: Cut out the *President Lincoln* flap book. Apply glue to the gray center section and attach at the bottom of the page. Under each flap, write a summary.

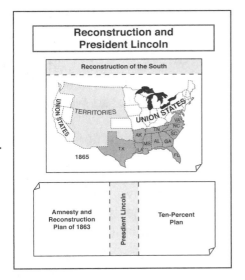

Demonstrate and Reflect on What You Have Learned

At his first public appearance after the war, President Lincoln asked the band to play "Dixie," a favorite Southern song. "I have always thought 'Dixie' one of the best tunes I have ever heard," he said. Think about what you learned from the reading selection. Why do you think Lincoln made this request? Write the answer in your interactive notebook. Support your opinion with specific details or examples.

Lincoln visited Richmond, Virginia, on April 4, 1865, after it was abandoned by the Confederate Army.

Key Details

Reconstruction and President Lincoln

When the American Civil War ended in 1865, over 620,000 Americans had died. Thousands more had been wounded or were seriously ill. Men returned to their families blind, deaf, or missing arms and legs. Families lost sons, fathers, brothers, and husbands. Over 250,000 Confederate soldiers had been killed. Another 37,000 African Americans had died fighting for their freedom.

Reconstruction Era

The Civil War caused billions of dollars of damage to the Southern states. The South was in shambles. Property damage was so extensive in the South that some areas took years to recover. The Union Army had destroyed homes, businesses, farm animals, and fields. The Confederate Army had also destroyed many resources to keep them out of Union hands. Cities were in ruins; homes had been burned, crops had been destroyed, and railroad lines were torn up. The Southern economy was ruined. Confederate money was worthless. The social system that had existed in the South before the Civil War had been destroyed. The formerly enslaved people were free, but free to do what? Most had no land, no homes, no education, no money, and no opportunities.

The destruction forced the South to begin a period of reconstruction. Most Northerners believed that it was necessary because of conditions in the Southern states, but few agreed on what should be done. They also disagreed about how to ensure the freedom and civil rights of formerly enslaved people. With the Confederate government powerless, the North clearly had to deal with the situation. **Reconstruction**, or the time of rebuilding the Southern states after the Civil War, lasted from 1865 to 1877.

Lincoln's Vision for Reconstruction

After the major Union victories at the battles of Gettysburg and Vicksburg in 1863, President Abraham Lincoln began preparing his plan for Reconstruction to reunify the North and South after the war's end. Because Lincoln believed that the South had never legally seceded from the Union, his plan for Reconstruction was based on forgiveness. He thus issued the **Proclamation of Amnesty and Reconstruction** on December 8, 1863, to announce his plan to reunite the once-united states. Lincoln hoped that the proclamation would rally Northern support for the war and persuade weary Confederate soldiers to surrender. It gave a full pardon for and restoration of property to Southerners who had participated in the war except for the highest Confederate officials and military leaders. The plan allowed for new state governments to be formed in the South. The plan also dealt with the problem of housing, clothing, and feeding the millions of enslaved people who would be freed.

Lincoln's Ten-Percent Plan

President Lincoln's blueprint for Reconstruction included the **Ten-Percent Plan**. The plan required that ten percent of the voters in a state that had joined the Confederacy must take an oath of loyalty to the United States. Then the state could send representatives to Congress, and the state would be readmitted to the Union.

Reconstruction and President Lincoln

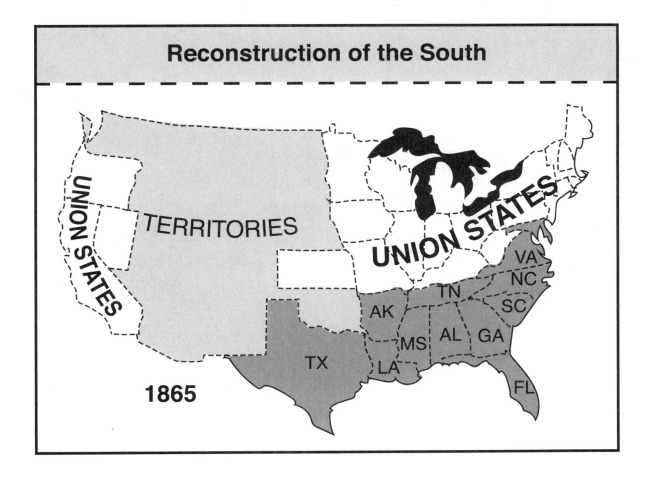

Reconstruction of the South

TERRITORIES

UNION STATES

UNION STATES

UNION STATES

VA
NC
TN
SC
AK
AL   GA
MS
TX   LA
FL

1865

| Amnesty and Reconstruction Plan of 1863 | President Lincoln | Ten-Percent Plan |

Student Instructions: The Freedmen's Bureau

Materials Needed

Glue, scissors, colored pencils

How to Create a Right-hand Interactive Notebook Page

Read the Key Details page. Then cut out the box and attach it to the right-hand page of your interactive notebook. Use what you have learned to create the left-hand page.

How to Create a Left-hand Interactive Notebook Page

Complete the following steps to create the left-hand page of your interactive notebook. Use lots of color.

Step 1: Cut out the title and glue it to the top of the notebook page.

Step 2: Cut out the four *Question* pieces. Apply glue to the back of the gray tabs and attach them below the title.

Step 3: Under each flap, answer the question.

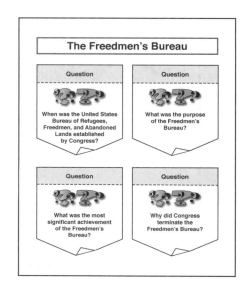

Demonstrate and Reflect on What You Have Learned

　　　　Think about what you learned from the reading selection. In your interactive notebook, write five facts about the public education system established by the Freedmen's Bureau for those who were formerly enslaved.

A Freedmen's Bureau school in the South

Key Details

The Freedmen's Bureau

One of the challenges of rebuilding the South after the Civil War was how to help the 4 million **freedmen**, or formerly enslaved persons, transition from slavery to freedom. Most had no property, few skills, and nowhere to go. President Abraham Lincoln developed a plan to deal with the problem. He proposed creating a federal agency to assist those who had been enslaved.

Freedmen's Bureau

The United States Bureau of Refugees, Freedmen, and Abandoned Lands was established by Congress on March 3, 1865, two months before Robert E. Lee and the Confederate Army surrendered to Ulysses S. Grant at Appomattox Court House in Virginia. The new agency was placed under the authority of the United States War Department. It had the authority to operate for the duration of the war and for one year after. Many of the men who ran the bureau were Civil War soldiers.

Purpose of the Freedmen's Bureau

By the time the Civil War ended, the **bureau**, or agency, commonly referred to as the **Freedmen's Bureau**, had opened offices throughout the South and had begun providing relief to all Southerners. It provided food, shelter, clothing, and medical services. It opened hospitals and provided medical assistance to millions of people.

The agency had the authority to give land confiscated or abandoned during the war to formerly enslaved people so they could have a home, grow food, and take care of themselves. However, President Andrew Johnson, who took over after Lincoln's death, opposed that effort. He gave the abandoned lands to white Southerners pardoned for taking part in the war.

Most Significant Achievement of the Freedmen's Bureau

Old Main Building at Howard University, c. 1900

The most significant achievement of the bureau was the establishment of a public education system in the South for formerly enslaved people. It opened more than 1,000 schools. Students from 5 to 90 years old attended the schools. These schools ran seven days a week, with classes from early morning to late at night. The bureau spent over $400,000 to establish teacher training centers.

Trade schools like Hampton Institute in Virginia opened to prepare the formerly enslaved for skilled labor jobs. Colleges for Black students were also established, like Howard University in Washington, D.C., Atlanta University in Atlanta, Georgia, and Fisk University in Nashville, Tennessee.

Congress Terminates the Freedmen's Bureau

Although it did much to help the formerly enslaved people of the South, the bureau had inadequate funds and poorly trained personnel. As more and more of the power was drained away from this agency, it eventually did little more than oversee sharecropping arrangements. Congress terminated the bureau in July 1872.

The Freedmen's Bureau

Question

When was the United States Bureau of Refugees, Freedmen, and Abandoned Lands established by Congress?

Question

What was the purpose of the Freedmen's Bureau?

Question

What was the most significant achievement of the Freedmen's Bureau?

Question

Why did Congress terminate the Freedmen's Bureau?

Student Instructions: Assassination of President Lincoln

Materials Needed

Glue, scissors, colored pencils

How to Create a Right-hand Interactive Notebook Page

Read the Key Details page. Then cut out the page and attach it to the right-hand page of your interactive notebook. Use what you have learned to create the left-hand page.

How to Create a Left-hand Interactive Notebook Page

Complete the following steps to create the left-hand page of your interactive notebook. Use lots of color.

Step 1: Cut out the title and glue it to the top of the notebook page.

Step 2: Fill in the event for each date on the *Timeline* chart. Cut out the chart. Apply glue to the back and attach it below the title.

Assassination of President Lincoln		
Timeline		
April 9, 1865	April 14, 1865	April 26, 1865
Event Summary	Event Summary	Event Summary

Demonstrate and Reflect on What You Have Learned

The news of the fall of Richmond, the Confederate capital, and General Robert E. Lee's surrender to General Ulysses S. Grant at Appomattox Court House hit John Wilkes Booth hard. The idea came to him of killing President Lincoln, Vice President Andrew Johnson, and Secretary of State Seward. Booth called his little band of followers together and handed out assignments to Lewis Powell, David Herold, and George Atzerodt. Use the Internet or other reference sources to research Booth's plot to kill members of Lincoln's administration. What was the outcome of the assassination attempts? Write the answer in your interactive notebook. Support your answer with specific details or examples.

John Wilkes Booth was an actor and Confederate sympathizer.

Key Details

Assassination of President Lincoln

President Abraham Lincoln was re-elected to office on November 8, 1864. On April 9, 1865, General Robert E. Lee and the Confederate Army surrendered at Appomattox Court House, Virginia, and the Civil War effectively came to an end.

John Wilkes Booth

Many Southerners blamed President Lincoln for the war. Actor John Wilkes Booth was one of them. He was a Confederate **sympathizer**, someone who supported the cause but didn't actually fight in the war. Booth plotted to **assassinate**, or kill, Lincoln, Vice President Andrew Johnson, and Secretary of State William Steward. Booth hoped to throw the Union government into chaos, and perhaps the Confederacy could then reorganize resistance.

Lincoln Assassinated at Ford's Theatre

On April 14, 1864, President and Mrs. Lincoln and their guests Major Henry Rathbone and his fiancée, Clara Harris, arrived at Ford's Theatre. The bodyguard for the evening, John Parker, left his seat outside the presidential box to find a seat where he could watch the play.

Booth entered the theater after the play had begun, found the president's box unguarded, and came up behind Lincoln with a Derringer pistol in one hand and a knife in the other. He shot the president at point blank range and prepared to leap from the box. Rathbone grabbed his arm, and Booth slashed him with the knife. Booth jumped from the box. Tradition has it that as he fell, he caught his spur in the flag material draped from the railing, landed off-balance, and broke his leg. He yelled "Sic Semper Tyrannis" (Latin for "Thus always to tyrants"), hobbled out the stage door, and rode off on his horse. However, after examining eyewitness accounts, it appears Booth may have broken his leg later in his escape when his horse fell on him.

The first doctor to arrive was Charles Leale, a young army surgeon. By then, Lincoln was unconscious and barely breathing. After examining him, Leale told the others, "His wound is mortal. It is impossible for him to recover."

Carefully, the president was carried across the street to Peterson's Boardinghouse. Doctors made two unsuccessful attempts to remove the bullet. Lincoln never regained consciousness. He died the following morning at 7:22 A.M.

Fate of the Conspirators

After Booth escaped from Ford's Theatre, he met **conspirator**, or fellow plotter, David Herold. They rode to a tavern owned by Mary Surratt, where they had met on several occasions to discuss their plans. They went on to the home of Dr. Mudd, a Southern sympathizer Booth knew. Dr. Mudd set Booth's broken leg and let Booth and Herold spend the night.

Rewards offered for the capture of the conspirators

The next day, Booth and Herold fled south. Federal authorities caught up with them in a storage shed near Port Royal, Virginia, on April 26, 1865. Herold surrendered; Booth refused. The shed was set on fire; Booth was shot and killed.

The authorities arrested the other conspirators. Several, including David Herold and Mary Surratt, were hung on July 7, 1865. Dr. Mudd was sentenced to life in prison.

Assassination of President Lincoln

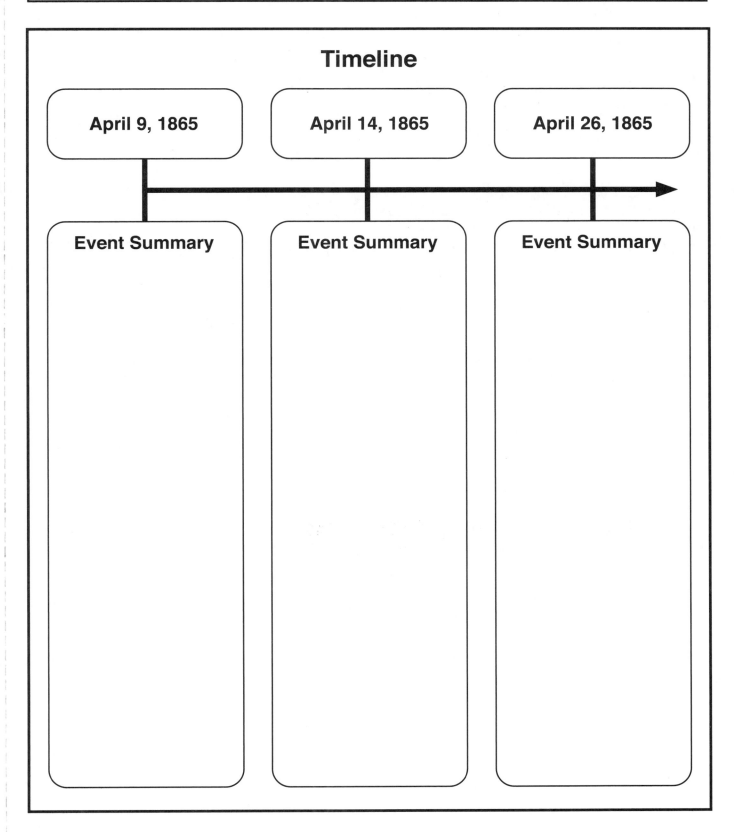

Timeline

April 9, 1865	April 14, 1865	April 26, 1865
Event Summary	**Event Summary**	**Event Summary**

Student Instructions: Andrew Johnson Becomes President

Materials Needed

Glue, scissors, colored pencils

How to Create a Right-hand Interactive Notebook Page

Read the Key Details page. Then cut out the page and attach it to the right-hand page of your interactive notebook. Use what you have learned to create the left-hand page.

How to Create a Left-hand Interactive Notebook Page

Complete the following steps to create the left-hand page of your interactive notebook. Use lots of color.

Step 1: Cut out the title and glue it to the top of the notebook page.

Step 2: Complete the *The Veto President, Tenure of Office Act,* and *Impeachment* pieces. Briefly describe each event in President Andrew Johnson's term in office.

Step 3: Cut out the three pieces. Apply glue to the back of each piece and attach them below the title.

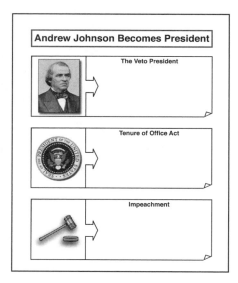

Demonstrate and Reflect on What You Have Learned

Three presidents have been impeached by Congress. Use the Internet or other reference sources to learn more about the charges and trials. Draw a chart like the one below in your interactive notebook. Use your research to complete the chart.

President	Year	Charges	Results

Key Details

Andrew Johnson Becomes President

A strong Democrat, Andrew Johnson moved up the political ladder from alderman to United States senator. When Tennessee left the Union, Johnson remained in the Senate. After the Union army moved into Tennessee, President Abraham Lincoln appointed Johnson military governor of the state. In 1864, he was chosen for Lincoln's vice president to win support from border-state Democrats.

Trouble for Johnson

After President Abraham Lincoln's death, on April 15, 1865, Andrew Johnson, the vice president, took the oath of office and became the nation's seventeenth president. He talked about following a hard line toward the South, which appealed to a group of Republicans in Congress who thought Lincoln had been too soft on the South. Lincoln had believed that a **lenient** Reconstruction was the best way to mend the wounds of the war. His goal was to unite the states under one government. He did not want to punish the South for the war. When Johnson took over as president, his plan for Reconstruction included the continuation of Lincoln's plan. When Congress saw Johnson following Lincoln's lenient policies, they turned against the president.

Johnson did not favor equal rights for **freedmen**, or formerly enslaved people, and offered them no role in Reconstruction. Johnson vetoed the **Freedmen's Bureau Bill** and the **Civil Rights Act**. Both were intended to protect the rights of the formerly enslaved. He vetoed the **Fourteenth Amendment** to the Constitution, which guaranteed citizenship rights to anyone born in the United States. The term **veto** means the president prevents a bill passed by Congress from becoming law. Congress voted to **override the vetoes**, or to pass the bills over the president's objections. Johnson used the veto 29 times. He vetoed so many bills that he became known as the **Veto President**. Congress felt that he was abusing his power.

Congress became concerned with Johnson's lenient policies toward the South. One member of Johnson's cabinet, Secretary of War Edwin Stanton, agreed with the Republican Congress. Johnson notified Congress that he was dismissing Stanton. On March 3, 1867, the **Tenure of Office Act** was enacted. It stated that the president could not remove a Cabinet member he had appointed without the consent of the Senate. The act had been specifically designed by Congress to protect Secretary of War Edwin Stanton from dismissal by President Andrew Johnson.

Johnson Is Impeached

The crisis over the dismissal of Edwin Stanton led to Johnson's impeachment. **Impeachment** is when an elected federal official, in this case the president, is brought up on charges of misconduct by the House of Representatives. On February 24, 1868, the House voted 126–47 that Johnson be impeached. He was the first president of the United States to ever be impeached. The next step in the process was for a trial to take place in the Senate to see if the president was to be removed from office. After the trial, the motion to remove Johnson from office failed by a single vote. Johnson finished his term as president. However, he and Congress continued to be at odds.

Andrew Johnson Becomes President

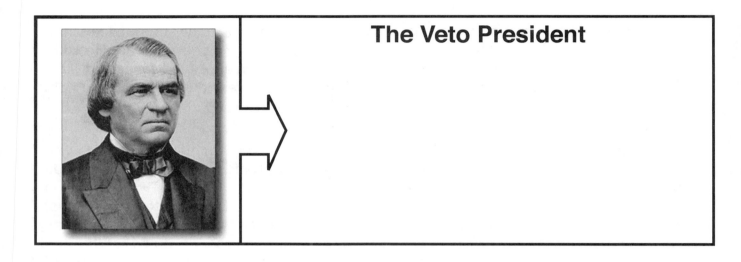

The Veto President

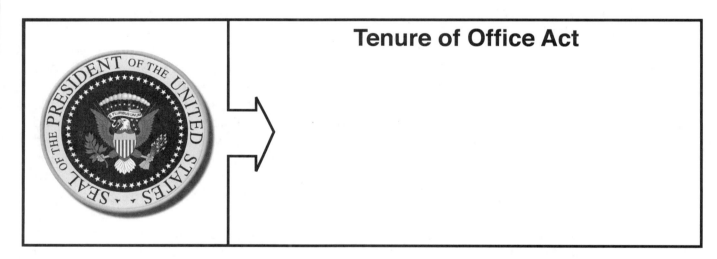

Tenure of Office Act

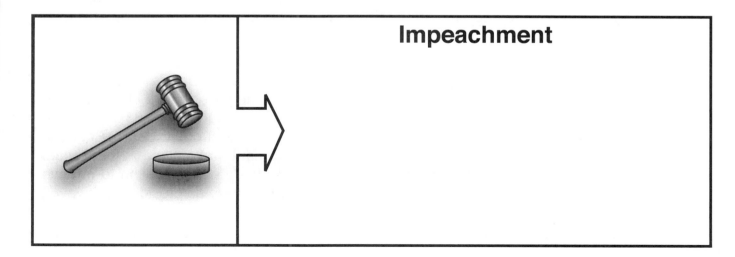

Impeachment

Student Instructions: A Plan for Restoration

Materials Needed

Glue, scissors, colored pencils

How to Create a Right-hand Interactive Notebook Page

Read the Key Details page. Then cut out the section and attach it to the right-hand page of your interactive notebook. Use what you have learned to create the left-hand page.

How to Create a Left-hand Interactive Notebook Page

Complete the following steps to create the left-hand page of your interactive notebook. Use lots of color.

Step 1: Cut out the title and glue it to the top of the notebook page.

Step 2: Cut out the *Reconstruction Plans* flap book. Cut on the solid line to create two flaps. Apply glue to the back of the gray tab and attach it below the title. Under the flaps, explain President Andrew Johnson's plan.

Step 3: Cut out the *Definitions* flap book. Cut on the solid lines to create four flaps. Apply glue to the back of the gray center section and attach it at the bottom of the page. Under each flap, write a definition.

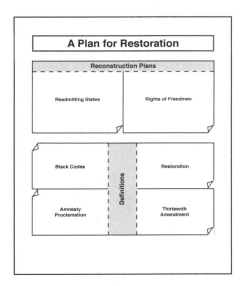

Demonstrate and Reflect on What You Have Learned

    Freedmen was a term used in the reading selection. Use the Internet or other resources to research the term. What is the meaning of freedmen? What problems did freedmen face after the Civil War? Write the answers in your interactive notebook. Support your answers with specific details or examples.

After the Civil War, the Freedmen's Bureau opened more than 1,000 schools for the formerly enslaved.

A Plan for Restoration

The rebuilding of the South after the Civil War occurred from 1865 to 1877. This period of time was known as **Reconstruction**. President Abraham Lincoln wanted to help those who had been freed from slavery, rebuild the economy of the South, and unite the Southern and Northern states under one government. However, Lincoln was assassinated at the end of the war, and he never had a chance to implement his plan for Reconstruction.

Johnson's Plan for Reconstruction

Vice President Andrew Johnson took over as president after President Abraham Lincoln's death in 1865. Johnson planned to continue Lincoln's lenient policies toward the South. Like Lincoln, his goal was to quickly unite the Southern and Northern states under one government. He did not want to punish the South for the war. He believed in the rights of states to regulate their own affairs. Johnson called his plan for rebuilding the south **Restoration**.

The first thing Johnson did was issue an **amnesty proclamation**, or announcement of presidential pardons. On May 29, 1865, following the end of the Civil War, Johnson gave some former Confederates amnesty upon their taking an oath to defend the Constitution and the Union and to obey all federal laws. Later proclamations would extend amnesty to more groups of Confederates until December 25, 1868, when President Johnson issued his final proclamation, which pardoned all who had participated in the rebellion.

Johnson planned to allow the Confederate states to form new governments and rejoin the Union as quickly as possible. He required only that the Southern states agree that slavery and secession were illegal to be readmitted to the Union. Southern states were then allowed to elect their own leaders and to set up new state governments.

Northern members of Congress refused to allow Southerners to participate in the United States Congress until their states had been readmitted to the Union. To be readmitted, they required states to ratify the **Thirteenth Amendment**, which Congress had passed in January 1865. The amendment abolished slavery in the United States. By the end of 1865, all but one of the former Confederate states were ready to rejoin the Union. Johnson declared the goal of national unity achieved and Reconstruction completed.

Rights of Freedmen

Johnson's plan for Reconstruction did not include the involvement of formerly enslaved people in government. Johnson did not favor equal rights for Blacks and offered them no role in Reconstruction. Even though Blacks were legally free, they were allowed very little freedom. **Freedmen**, or people who had been freed from slavery, were not allowed to vote or hold public office.

Johnson believed states should manage their own transition from slavery to freedom. After receiving pardons, many former Confederate leaders were elected to high positions in the states and to Congress. The new lawmakers passed laws known as the **Black Codes**, which limited the rights of Black people.

22

A Plan for Restoration

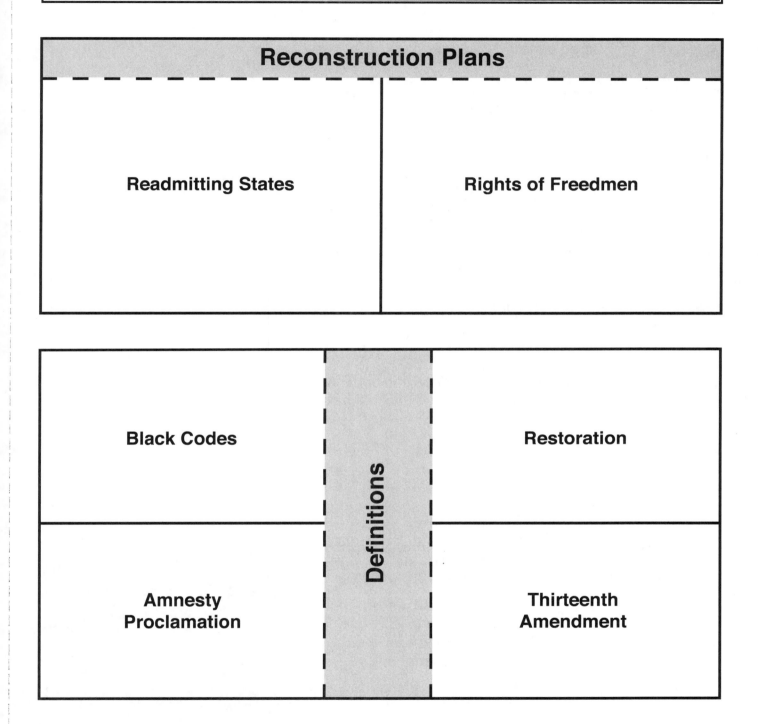

Reconstruction Plans

Readmitting States

Rights of Freedmen

Black Codes

Definitions

Restoration

Amnesty Proclamation

Thirteenth Amendment

Student Instructions: The Civil Rights Act of 1866

Materials Needed

Glue, scissors, colored pencils

How to Create a Right-hand Interactive Notebook Page

Read the Key Details page. Then cut out the page and attach it to the right-hand page of your interactive notebook. Use what you have learned to create the left-hand page.

How to Create a Left-hand Interactive Notebook Page

Complete the following steps to create the left-hand page of your interactive notebook. Use lots of color.

Step 1: Cut out the title and glue it to the top of the notebook page.

Step 2: Cut out the *Civil Rights Act of 1866* flap book. Apply glue to the gray center section and attach it below the title.

Step 3: Under each flap, write a summary.

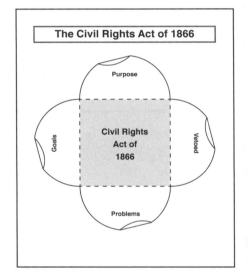

Demonstrate and Reflect on What You Have Learned

Think about what you have learned from the reading selection. Use the information to create a news article about the Civil Rights Act of 1866. Remember to answer the questions: who, what, where, when, why, and how? Support the article with specific details or examples.

Mural in the U.S. Capitol Building commemorating the Civil Rights Act of 1866.

Key Details

The Civil Rights Act of 1866

The 13 British colonies became the 13 states of the United States in 1776. By 1865, the country had survived over a century of slavery and four years of Civil War to end slavery. The nation now struggled with the idea of equality for formerly enslaved people.

Civil Rights Act of 1866

The Civil Rights Bill was written by Senator Lyman for the purpose of giving **freedmen**, or those freed from slavery, certain basic **civil rights**, or equal protection under the law regardless of race or color. Many members of Congress felt that this was a necessary step after the abolishment of slavery and end of the Civil War.

President Andrew Johnson did not support the Civil Rights Act, which if passed would become a federal law that all states would be required to enforce. He had always been a firm believer in the rights of states to regulate their own affairs. He stated:

In all our history, in all our experience as a people living under Federal and State law, no such system as that contemplated by the details of this bill has ever before been proposed or adopted. They establish for the security of the colored race safeguards which go indefinitely beyond any that The General Government has ever provided for the white race. In fact, the distinction of race and color is by the bill made to operate in favor of the colored against the white race. They interfere with the municipal legislation of states; with relations existing exclusively between a state and its citizens or between inhabitants of the same State; an absorption and assumption of power by the General Government which, if acquiesced in must sap and destroy our federative system of lined power, break down the barriers which preserve the rights of the states.

President Johnson **vetoed**, or rejected, the bill. Congress overrode Johnson's veto, and the Civil Rights Act was passed by Congress on April 9, 1866. When Johnson learned that Congress had overridden his veto, he claimed that Congress was filled with traitors.

Goals of the Civil Rights Act

The Civil Rights Act was a law that accomplished three major goals. The act established that all males born in the United States were considered citizens. Before, only white males were considered citizens. It defined the rights of citizenship. They included the right to own, buy, and sell property, the right to use the justice system and file lawsuits, and the right to make and carry out contracts. The law made it illegal to deny someone these rights based on race or color. Persons who denied these rights to formerly enslaved people could be fined or imprisoned.

Problems With the Civil Rights Act

The Civil Rights Act guaranteed all citizens certain civil rights. However, it did not address **political rights**. It did not give freedmen the right to vote or the right to hold public office.

The Civil Rights Act of 1866

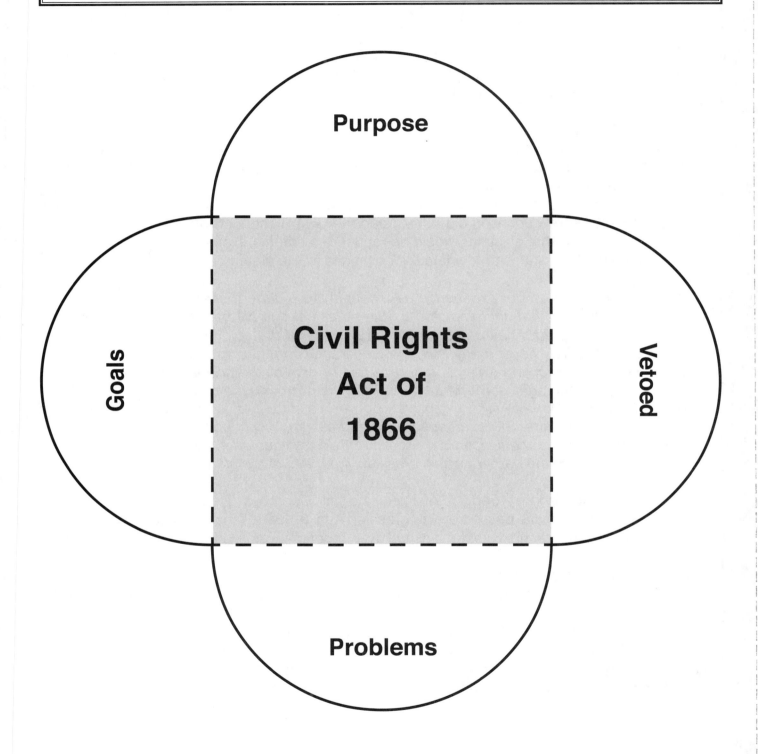

Purpose

Goals

Civil Rights Act of 1866

Vetoed

Problems

Student Instructions: Black Codes

Materials Needed

Glue, scissors, colored pencils

How to Create a Right-hand Interactive Notebook Page

Read the Key Details page. Then cut out the page and attach it to the right-hand page of your interactive notebook. Use what you have learned to create the left-hand page.

How to Create a Left-hand Interactive Notebook Page

Complete the following steps to create the left-hand page of your interactive notebook. Use lots of color.

Step 1: Cut out the title and glue it to the top of the notebook page.

Step 2: Cut out the *Southern State Legislatures* flap book. Cut on the solid lines to create three flaps. Apply glue to the back of the gray tab and attach it below the title. Under each flap, write a summary.

Step 3: Cut out the *Consequences of Black Codes* flap book. Cut on the solid lines to create two flaps. Apply glue to the back of the gray tab and attach it at the bottom of the page. Under each flap, explain the consequences of the Black Codes.

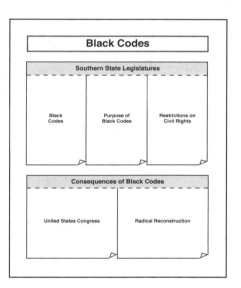

Demonstrate and Reflect on What You Have Learned

Vagrancy laws were enacted during the Reconstruction Era. Think about what you learned in the reading selection. What is a vagrant? What was the penalty for vagrancy during Reconstruction? How did these laws target formerly enslaved people? Write your answers in your interactive notebook. Support your answers with specific details or examples.

Key Details

Black Codes

President Andrew Johnson had always been a firm believer in the rights of states to regulate their own affairs. Under his Restoration plan, Southern states were allowed to elect their own leaders and to set up new state governments. As a result, many former Confederate leaders were elected to high positions in the South and in Congress.

Black Codes

In 1865 and early 1866, the new Southern state **legislatures**, or lawmaking bodies, passed a series of laws based on the slave codes that had been in effect since early colonial days. The slave codes were based on the idea that an enslaved person was property, not a person, and had few or no legal rights. These new laws were called the **Black Codes**. These laws were intended to keep the social situation in the South as close as possible to what it had been before the Civil War. Even though formerly enslaved people were legally free, they were allowed very little freedom.

Purpose of Black Codes

The Black Codes were designed to continue providing cheap sources of labor for Southerners and were based on the belief that Black people were inferior beings. **Freedmen**, or formerly enslaved people, were required to sign yearly labor contracts, often with their former owners. If the freedmen were unemployed and without a permanent residence, they could be declared **vagrants**. Vagrants were arrested and fined. If unable to pay, they were forced to work for white employers to pay off the fine.

Black Codes Restricted Civil Rights

Black Codes limited the civil rights of freedmen. **Civil rights** are opportunities, treatment, and protection everyone is guaranteed under the law. Black Codes restricted freedmen from
- owning or renting farms
- living in many cities
- owning certain businesses
- working in specific trades in some states
- carrying firearms
- meeting in unsupervised groups
- testifying in court
- voting or holding public office
- traveling without permission from the government

Results

The situation in the South prompted the United States Congress to take strong federal measures to establish laws that guaranteed the rights of Black people. By some, these measures were considered **radical**, or extreme. This new phase in Reconstruction became known as **Radical Reconstruction**. The federal government eliminated the Black Codes and limited the power of the state governments in the South.

Black Codes

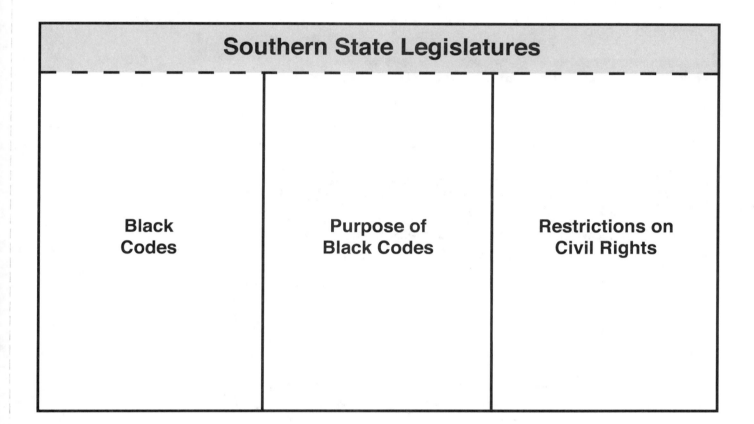

Southern State Legislatures

Black Codes

Purpose of Black Codes

Restrictions on Civil Rights

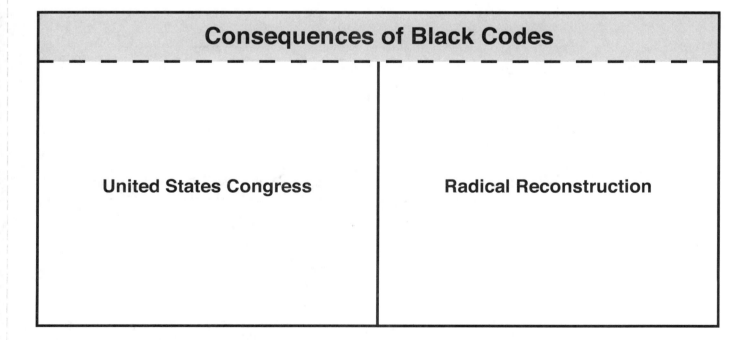

Consequences of Black Codes

United States Congress

Radical Reconstruction

Student Instructions: Congressional Reconstruction Plan

Materials Needed

Glue, scissors, colored pencils

How to Create a Right-hand Interactive Notebook Page

Read the Key Details page. Then cut out the page and attach it to the right-hand page of your interactive notebook. Use what you have learned to create the left-hand page.

How to Create a Left-hand Interactive Notebook Page

Complete the following steps to create the left-hand page of your interactive notebook. Use lots of color.

Step 1: Cut out the title and glue it to the top of the notebook page.

Step 2: Complete each panel of the chart. Cut out the chart. Apply glue to the back and attach it below the title.

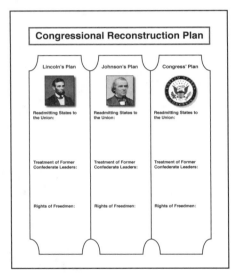

Demonstrate and Reflect on What You Have Learned

Think about what you learned from the reading selection. Which Reconstruction plan do you think was the most successful or could have been the most successful if allowed to continue? Write the answer in your interactive notebook. Support your answer with specific details or examples.

This Reconstruction Era photograph shows the ruins of Richmond, Virginia, at the end of the Civil War.

Key Details

Congressional Reconstruction Plan

There were many different ideas about how Reconstruction should be handled. Most debates involved two opposing viewpoints: those of the presidents and the U.S. Congress.

Presidential Reconstruction Plans

President Abraham Lincoln had a simple plan for reuniting the nation known as the **Ten-Percent Plan**. The purpose of the plan proposed by Lincoln was to quickly readmit the Southern states to the Union. The plan made it easy for Confederate states to form new governments and rejoin the Union. The new state governments had to ratify the **Thirteenth Amendment** abolishing slavery. It also required that ten percent of the voters in a state take an oath of loyalty to the United States, and Lincoln offered a pardon to all Southerners except for Confederate leaders.

Lincoln wanted to help house, clothe, and feed the millions of formerly enslaved people, so he established the Freedmen's Bureau to assist them. However, he was not in favor of Blacks and whites having the same rights.

When Lincoln was assassinated in April 1865, Andrew Johnson then became president. His plan was considered by Congress even more lenient than President Lincoln's plan. States that disowned their act of secession and ratified the Thirteenth Amendment would be readmitted to the Union. He offered pardons to all Southerners including Confederate leaders who pledged allegiance to the Union and who agreed to the abolition of slavery. Johnson did not favor equal rights for formerly enslaved people and offered them no role in Reconstruction. He opposed the Freedmen's Bureau, the Civil Rights Act of 1866, and the **Fourteenth Amendment**, which granted citizenship and equal civil and legal rights to anyone born in the United States.

Congressional Plan

Republicans in Congress felt the Presidential Plans for Reconstruction were too lenient and supported a stricter plan. These Republicans were called **Radicals**. In 1867, the Radical Republicans took control of the United States Congress. The period that followed was called **Radical Reconstruction**. During this time, Congress passed a series of **Reconstruction Acts** dividing the South into five military districts to be in effect until the states adopted new constitutions and were readmitted to the Union. Congress banned everyone who formerly had held office in one of the states that seceded from the Union during the Civil War from voting or holding state or federal office.

Before former Confederate states could be readmitted to the Union, Congress declared they must meet certain requirements. A majority of white male citizens had to take an oath, swearing that they had never been disloyal to the United States. States were to rewrite their state constitutions removing **Black Codes**, which were laws designed to limit the freedom of Black people. Also, Southern states had to ratify the Thirteenth and Fourteenth Amendments, and Black men were to be allowed to vote.

 CD-405069 © Mark Twain Media, Inc., Publishers 31

Congressional Reconstruction Plan

Lincoln's Plan

Readmitting States to the Union:

Treatment of Former Confederate Leaders:

Rights of Freedmen:

Johnson's Plan

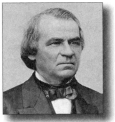

Readmitting States to the Union:

Treatment of Former Confederate Leaders:

Rights of Freedmen:

Congress' Plan

Readmitting States to the Union:

Treatment of Former Confederate Leaders:

Rights of Freedmen:

Student Instructions: Reconstruction Acts

Materials Needed

Glue, scissors, colored pencils

How to Create a Right-hand Interactive Notebook Page

Read the Key Details page. Then cut out the page and attach it to the right-hand page of your interactive notebook. Use what you have learned to create the left-hand page.

How to Create a Left-hand Interactive Notebook Page

Complete the following steps to create the left-hand page of your interactive notebook. Use lots of color.

Step 1: Cut out the title and glue it to the top of the notebook page.

Step 2: Cut out the *What Does it Mean?* flap book. Apply glue to the back of the gray center section and attach it below the title. Under each flap, write the definition.

Step 3: Cut out the *Military Reconstruction Districts, 1867* flap piece. Apply glue to the back of the gray tab and attach it at the bottom of the page. Under the flap, summarize the four Reconstruction Acts.

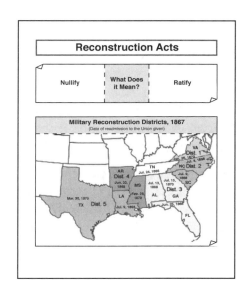

Demonstrate and Reflect on What You Have Learned

Slavery was officially abolished after the Civil War by the Thirteenth Amendment to the Constitution. That didn't mean, however, that the war or the amendment put an end to the problems of the African Americans living in the South. Use the Internet or other reference sources to research the Reconstruction Era. In your interactive notebook, list five concerns a formerly enslaved person might have had during the Reconstruction Era.

The first African-American senator and representatives served in the 41st and 42nd Congress of the United States (1869–1873).

Key Details

Reconstruction Acts

To launch its new Reconstruction plan, the United States Congress passed four **Reconstruction Acts**. After meeting all the requirements of the new laws, the former Confederate states could be readmitted to the Union and send representatives to the United States Congress. Congress passed these laws over President Andrew Johnson's vetoes.

First Reconstruction Act

On March 2, 1867, Congress passed the first Reconstruction Act. The act **nullified**, or abolished, all Southern state governments and divided the Confederacy into five military districts. Government officials were removed from office and replaced by military commanders appointed by the United States Congress. Approximately 20,000 troops were placed in the South to enforce military rule. The five military districts were (1) Virginia, (2) North and South Carolina, (3) Georgia, Alabama, and Florida, (4) Mississippi and Arkansas, and (5) Texas and Louisiana. Tennessee was excluded because it had already **ratified**, or approved, the Thirteenth and Fourteenth Amendments and rejoined the Union in 1866.

The Reconstruction Act also called for new states to hold elections. Former Confederate leaders were not allowed to vote or hold office. Each state was required to write a new constitution, which needed to be approved by a majority of all voters in each state, including African-American men. Each state had to ratify the Thirteenth and Fourteenth Amendments prior to readmission to the Union.

Second Reconstruction Act

The second Reconstruction Act was passed on March 23, 1867. The act required voters to be registered; African-American men who met the requirements were to be included as voters, as well as white men. It placed the military commander of each Southern state in control of registration and voting in the Southern states. It required that every voter recite the registration oath promising their support to the Constitution and their obedience to the law.

Third Reconstruction Act

The third Reconstruction Act passed on July 19, 1867, basically restated the authority of the U.S. government to declare the Southern state governments illegal and to put military commanders in charge of the state governments and elections.

Fourth Reconstruction Act

On February 27, 1868, Congress passed the fourth and last Reconstruction Act. It changed the requirement for voter approval of a state constitution from a majority of all registered voters to a majority of the people who actually cast ballots in the election. Many white voters had registered and then refused to vote, making it impossible to get a majority of registered voters to approve. This new law made it much easier for states to ratify their new constitutions.

End of Military Rule

Military rule in the south lasted for 10 years. By 1870, all 11 states that had seceded from the Union had rewritten their constitutions and been readmitted. However, the last federal troops did not leave Louisiana until 1877.

Reconstruction Acts

Nullify	What Does it Mean?	Ratify

Military Reconstruction Districts, 1867
(Date of readmission to the Union given)

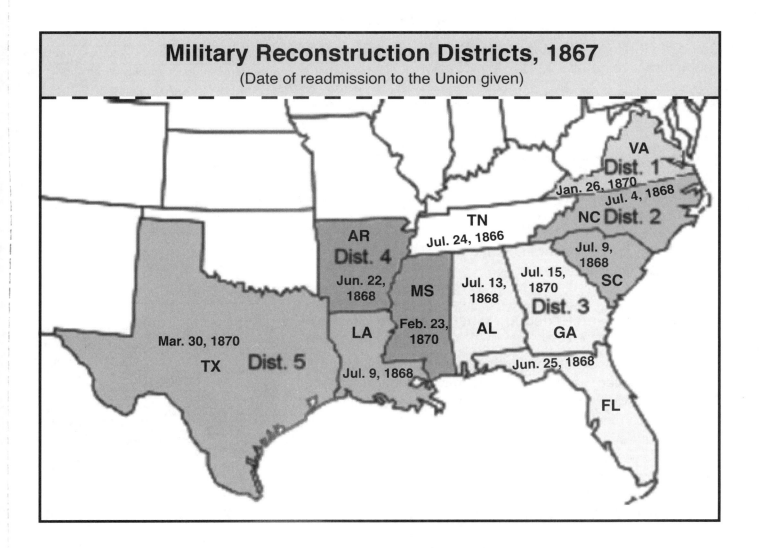

Student Instructions: Carpetbaggers and Scalawags

Materials Needed

Glue, scissors, colored pencils

How to Create a Right-hand Interactive Notebook Page

Read the Key Details page. Then cut out the page and attach it to the right-hand page of your interactive notebook. Use what you have learned to create the left-hand page.

How to Create a Left-hand Interactive Notebook Page

Complete the following steps to create the left-hand page of your interactive notebook. Use lots of color.

Step 1: Cut out the title and glue it to the top of the notebook page.

Step 2: Cut out the *Carpetbaggers* and *Scalawags* pockets. Fold back the gray tabs on the dotted lines. Apply glue to each of the gray tabs and attach the pockets below the title.

Step 3: Cut apart the word strips. Place each strip in the correct pocket.

Carpetbaggers and Scalawags
Carpetbaggers   Scalawags

Demonstrate and Reflect on What You Have Learned

This political cartoon first appeared in the illustrated newspaper called *Harper's Weekly* on November 9, 1872. Think about what you learned from the reading selection and then examine the illustration. Write the answers to the following questions in your interactive notebook.

1. Who created the cartoon?
2. Who does the man in the cartoon represent?
3. Is the man with the bags shown in a negative or positive light? Support your answer with specific details from the cartoon.
4. Who do the people in the crowd represent?
5. What do you think the cartoon is trying to reveal about Reconstruction? Support your answer with specific details or examples.

"The Man with the (Carpet) Bags"
political cartoon by Thomas Nast

Key Details

Carpetbaggers and Scalawags

The end of the Civil War was a time of great political change in the South. Government power switched from Democratic hands to Republican. The Reconstruction Acts of 1867 and 1868 set up guidelines for forming new state governments. These new governments were formed by a mixture of freedmen, Northerners who moved to the South, and Southerners who supported the Union.

Carpetbaggers

After the Civil War, a number of Northerners moved to the South. These Northerners were called **carpetbaggers** because they carried their belongings in bags made from scraps of carpet. Some were **opportunists**, looking for ways to exploit the political and financial problems of the South for their own gain. Many others came to improve education, provide medical assistance, and help restore Southern cities.

Many carpetbaggers were politicians who supported the Republicans. The United States Congress banned all former Confederate leaders and soldiers from voting or holding public office for a time. After one year of residence in the state, Northerners had the right to vote and hold office. Many transplanted Northerners then ran for and held political offices.

Some Northerners came to the South in quest of economic opportunities such as businessmen who wanted to make money by investing in the rebuilding. Others were ex-Union soldiers who wanted to settle in the South. They wanted to buy abandoned farmland and raise cotton.

A few Northerners were representatives of the Freedmen's Bureau and other federal Reconstruction agencies. Their goal was to improve living conditions and to promote education for the freedmen.

Scalawags

Southerners who cooperated with carpetbaggers were called **scalawags**. They were white Southerners who had not favored secession and who later supported the Reconstruction governments. Many were small farmers from the northern part of the South who had not owned slaves.

Resistant to Reconstruction

Reconstruction brought many changes that Southerners did not like. The North forced the South to live under military rule. New laws under Reconstruction required Southerners to treat Black people, whom they considered inferior, like equals.

The Southerners resented the new laws. They did not like Northerners moving in and trying to get rich off their troubles, and they considered Southerners who supported the Reconstruction as traitors to the South. In retaliation, some Southerners formed **vigilante groups**, secret terrorist organizations, such as the Ku Klux Klan and the Knights of the White Camelia. The groups wanted to regain white authority over the newly freed Black people. These groups tried to **intimidate**, or frighten, Blacks by threatening and carrying out violence.

Carpetbaggers and Scalawags

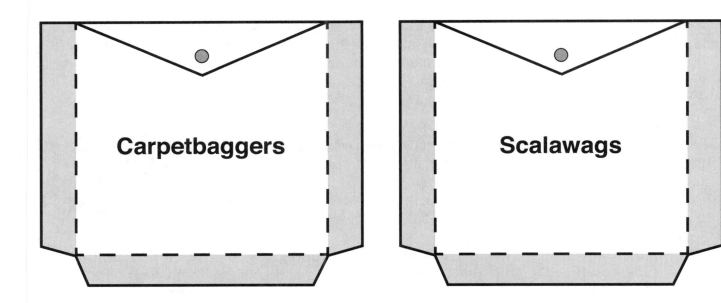

Southerners who supported the Union
Representatives of the Freedmen's Bureau
Northerners who carried bags made of scraps of carpet
Southerners who supported Reconstruction governments
Politicians, businessmen, and ex-Union soldiers who moved to the South
Southerners who had not owned slaves
Northerners who moved to the South during Reconstruction
Southerners who had not supported secession
Small farmers from the northern part of the South
Northerners who wanted to invest in rebuilding the South

Student Instructions: Forty Acres and a Mule

Materials Needed

Glue, scissors, colored pencils

How to Create a Right-hand Interactive Notebook Page

Read the Key Details page. Then cut out the page and attach it to the right-hand page of your interactive notebook. Use what you have learned to create the left-hand page.

How to Create a Left-hand Interactive Notebook Page

Complete the following steps to create the left-hand page of your interactive notebook. Use lots of color.

Step 1: Cut out the title and glue it to the top of the notebook page.

Step 2: Cut out the *Forty Acres and a Mule* flap book. Cut on the solid lines to create five flaps. Apply glue to the back of the gray center section. Attach the flap book below the title.

Step 3: Under each flap, explain the relationship to the "Forty Acres and a Mule" policy.

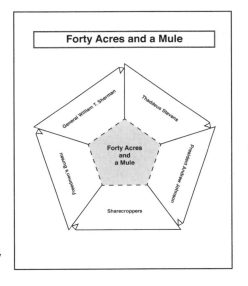

Demonstrate and Reflect on What You Have Learned

Forty Acres and Maybe a Mule, a book by Harriette Gillem Robinet, received the 1999 Scott O'Dell Award for historical fiction for children. Read the book. In your interactive notebook, write a book report for this historical fiction. Include the title, author, and a brief description of what happened in the book. This should only take a few sentences. Also give your opinion about what you thought of the book.

"Forty Acres and a Mule" was an expression that came to symbolize the expectations of newly freed Black people.

Key Details

Forty Acres and a Mule

"Forty Acres and a Mule" was an expression that came to symbolize the expectations of newly freed Black people. They believed the United States Congress would divide up Southern plantations and give parcels of land to formerly enslaved people.

General William T. Sherman

During the last months of the Civil War, thousands of formerly enslaved people followed General William T. Sherman and Union troops across Georgia and the Carolinas to the Atlantic Ocean. In January 1865, in an effort to address the problem of how to care for the refugees, Sherman issued **Special Field Order Number 15**. The order was a temporary plan granting each freed family 40 acres of land on the islands and coastal regions of Georgia. The Union Army also donated some of its mules to the formerly enslaved people.

Word of Sherman's order spread through the South. When the war ended three months later, many freedmen saw the "40 acres and a mule" policy of Sherman as proof that they would be able to own land.

United States Congress

In 1865 and 1866, the United States Congress debated how to help the South rebuild. **Thaddeus Stevens** urged Congress to adopt Sherman's "40 acres and a mule" policy.

Freedmen's Bureau

The **Freedmen's Bureau**, formally known as the Bureau of Refugees, Freedmen, and Abandoned Lands, was established before the end of the Civil War in 1865 by Congress. One of their tasks was to settle the freedmen on land confiscated or abandoned during the war.

President Andrew Johnson

Andrew Johnson became president in April 1865 following the assassination of Abraham Lincoln. He did not believe that freedmen should get free land. As one of the first acts of his Restoration plan in 1865, Johnson ordered all land under federal control be returned to the previous owners. The Freemen's Bureau had to inform the freedmen and whites living on the land that they could sign a labor contract with the previous landowners or be **evicted**, or removed, from the land. Both formerly enslaved people and poor white families became sharecroppers. Those who refused were forced out by the United States Army.

Sharecroppers

Most unskilled formerly enslaved people resumed work on plantations owned by whites as sharecroppers. The **sharecroppers** rented 10- to 50-acre plots. In exchange for land, a cabin, supplies, and a mule, sharecroppers agreed to raise a **cash crop** (usually cotton, tobacco, or rice). After the harvest, the landlord paid the sharecropper a share of the profits from the crop, usually one-third to one-half. In this way, the landowners got workers without having to pay wages, and the sharecroppers got land to work without having to buy it. However, any debts or expenses encountered by the sharecropper had to be taken out of their share of the profits. Most everything from food to shoes came from stores owned by the landlord. A year or two of bad crops could lead to the sharecropper being hopelessly in debt to the landowner.

CD-405069 © Mark Twain Media, Inc., Publishers

40

Forty Acres and a Mule

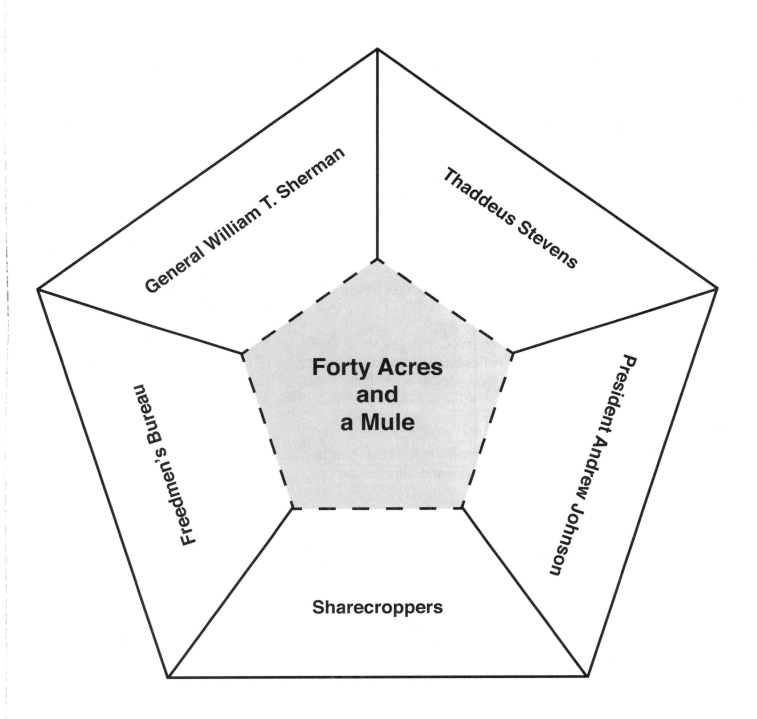

General William T. Sherman

Thaddeus Stevens

Freedmen's Bureau

Forty Acres and a Mule

President Andrew Johnson

Sharecroppers

Student Instructions: The Fourteenth Amendment

Materials Needed

Glue, scissors, colored pencils

How to Create a Right-hand Interactive Notebook Page

Read the Key Details page. Then cut out the page and attach it to the right-hand page of your interactive notebook. Use what you have learned to create the left-hand page.

How to Create a Left-hand Interactive Notebook Page

Complete the following steps to create the left-hand page of your interactive notebook. Use lots of color.

Step 1: Cut out the title and glue it to the top of the notebook page.

Step 2: Cut out the *14th Amendment Congress vs. President* flap book. Apply glue to the back of the gray section, and attach it below the title. Under each flap, describe the position of the Congress and the president on the Fourteenth Amendment.

Step 3: Complete the *14th Amendment* piece. Cut out the piece. Apply glue to the back, and attach it on the bottom part of the page.

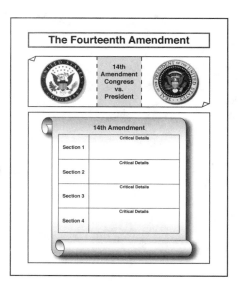

Demonstrate and Reflect on What You Have Learned

Before the Civil War, twelve amendments, or changes, to the United States Constitution had been ratified. Use the Internet or other reference sources to research each of the first twelve amendments. In your interactive notebook, create a chart with 12 rows like the one to the right. (You can make it as large as you need to for all the information.) Use your research to complete the chart.

Amendment	Summary
Amendment 1	
Amendment 2	
Amendment 3	
Amendment 4	
Amendment 5	

Key Details

The Fourteenth Amendment

During the Civil War, the Emancipation Proclamation freed enslaveed people in Southern states that had seceded from the Union. The **Thirteenth Amendment**, or change, to the United States Constitution abolished slavery in all states after the Civil War, but states still controlled the rights of the **freedmen**, or formerly enslaved people. During the Reconstruction Era, the **Fourteenth Amendment** was adopted, establishing the citizenship rights of formerly enslaved people and their descendants.

Congress

After the Civil War, many Southern states passed laws known as **Black Codes**. These laws restricted the rights of Black people. In 1866, the United States Congress went to work to remedy this situation. Representative Thaddeus Stevens helped write the Fourteenth Amendment to protect the civil rights of Black men, including the right to vote and own property.

The Fourteenth Amendment

The Fourteenth Amendment to the United States Constitution was **ratified**, or approved, on July 9, 1868. The amendment had several **sections**, or parts.

- **Section 1** of the amendment granted **citizenship** to all men who had been born or naturalized in the United States. However, women and Native Americans were not considered citizens and had none of the rights granted by the amendment. The amendment also guaranteed **due process** (right to a trial by a jury) and **equal protection** under the law to all citizens. The **Equal Protection Clause** prohibited states from implementing **Black Codes**, which were separate laws for Black people.
- **Section 2** of the amendment described how the state population would be counted in order to determine how many members of the House of Representatives each state would have. Prior to the amendment, formerly enslaved people were counted as three-fifths a person. The amendment required that all people be counted as a "whole number." States that prevented any adult male citizen from voting could lose part of their representation in Congress.
- **Section 3** of this amendment banned everyone who formerly held office in one of the states that seceded from the Union during the Civil War from voting or holding state or federal office.
- **Section 4** of the amendment prohibited the federal government or state governments from paying any Confederate war debt or from compensating former slave owners for the loss of their slaves.

President Andrew Johnson

President Johnson did not support the Fourteenth Amendment. He favored state control over voting rights, and he urged states to reject the amendment. Johnson **vetoed**, or did not approve of, the amendment and refused to sign it into law. Congress successfully overrode his veto, and the amendment was added to the Constitution in 1868 after being ratified by 28 states.

The Fourteenth Amendment

14th Amendment Congress vs. President

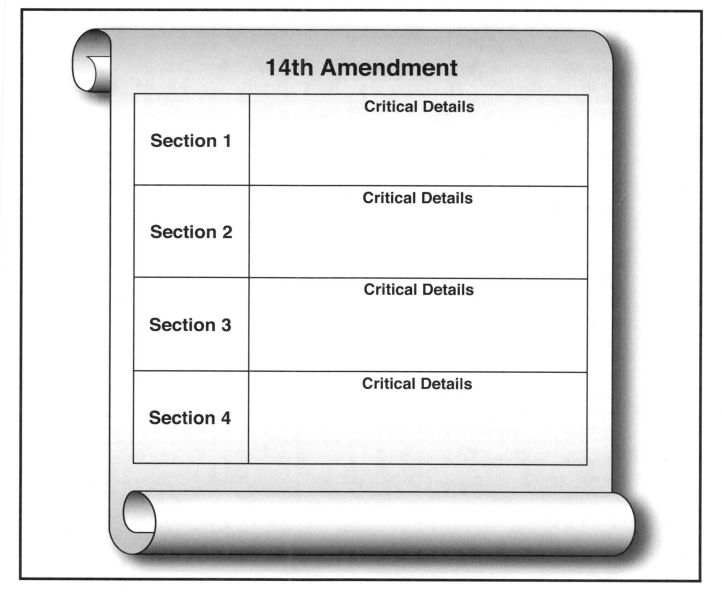

14th Amendment

	Critical Details
Section 1	Critical Details
Section 2	Critical Details
Section 3	Critical Details
Section 4	Critical Details

Student Instructions: Presidential Election of 1868

Materials Needed

Glue, scissors, colored pencils

How to Create a Right-hand Interactive Notebook Page

Read the Key Details page. Then cut out the page and attach it to the right-hand page of your interactive notebook. Use what you have learned to create the left-hand page.

How to Create a Left-hand Interactive Notebook Page

Complete the following steps to create the left-hand page of your interactive notebook. Use lots of color.

Step 1: Cut out the title and glue it to the top of the notebook page.

Step 2: Cut out the *Definitions* flap book. Cut on the solid line to create two flaps. Apply glue to the back of the gray tab and attach it below the title. Under each flap, write the definition.

Step 3: Cut out the *1868 Election* flap book. Cut on the solid lines to create four flaps. Apply glue to the back of the center section and attach it at the bottom of the page. Under each flap, write a summary.

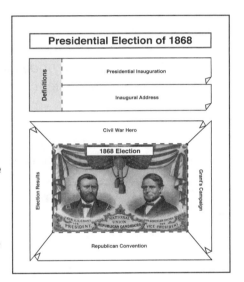

Demonstrate and Reflect on What You Have Learned

From George Washington to Franklin Roosevelt, the Presidential Inauguration Day was March 4. The Twentieth Amendment of the United States Constitution was ratified on January 23, 1933. This amendment changed the date for the incoming president and vice president to take the oath of office and start their new jobs. Use the Internet or other reference sources to research the Twentieth Amendment. What is the new inauguration date? Why was the change made? Write the answer in your interactive notebook.

Since 1801, most presidential inaugurations have been held in Washington D.C. at the Capitol Building.

Key Details

Presidential Election of 1868

Ulysses S. Grant was considered a war hero. His popularity soared after the Civil War, and he easily won the presential election of 1868 to become the 18th president of the United States.

War Hero

President Abraham Lincoln struggled to find a general to defeat Confederate General Robert E. Lee and the Confederate Army during the Civil War. In 1864, President Lincoln finally appointed Grant general-in-chief of the entire Union Army. Grant and Union troops eventually defeated General Lee. Lee and his soldiers surrendered at the village of Appomattox Court House, Virginia, on April 9, 1865.

Election of 1868

Other than a few months as the Secretary of War under President Johnson, Ulysses S. Grant had never held any political office. In fact, he had never run for an election at any level.

When the Republican Convention met in 1868 to nominate a candidate for president, every delegate voted for Grant on the first ballot. Grant's running mate was Speaker of the House Schuyler Colfax of Indiana. The Democrats nominated the governor of New York, Horatio Seymour, for president. Francis P. Blair of Missouri was chosen as his running mate.

Grant did not participate in the campaign, which was the custom at that time. His supporters would go out and drum up support for Grant. His campaign slogan was "Let Us have Peace." He remained at his home in Galena, Illinois, until the election results were known.

Election Results

Ulysses S. Grant won the popular vote by 300,000 and earned 214 of the 294 electoral votes. Two events helped Grant win the election. Many African Americans voted for the first time in that presidential election. Also, former Confederates, mostly Democrats, were denied the right to vote.

Grant was inaugurated the 18th president of the United States on March 4, 1869. The **presidential inauguration** is a ceremony where the president-elect becomes president. In his **inaugural address**, or speech,

Inauguration of President Grant, March 4, 1869

Grant urged ratification of the Fifteenth Amendment and expressed concern for proper treatment of Native Americans. He felt that they should be recognized as citizens and allowed to vote.

Re-election of Grant

Ulysses S. Grant was re-elected president in 1872. In 1880, Grant attempted to run for a third term as president. However, he did not win his party's nomination. Instead, James A. Garfield became the Republican candidate and went on to win the election.

Presidential Election of 1868

Definitions	Presidential Inauguration
	Inaugural Address

Civil War Hero

Election Results

1868 Election

Grant's Campaign

Republican Convention

Student Instructions: President Grant's First Term

Materials Needed

Glue, scissors, colored pencils

How to Create a Right-hand Interactive Notebook Page

Read the Key Details page. Then cut out the page and attach it to the right-hand page of your interactive notebook. Use what you have learned to create the left-hand page.

How to Create a Left-hand Interactive Notebook Page

Complete the following steps to create the left-hand page of your interactive notebook. Use lots of color.

Step 1: Cut out the title and glue it to the top of the notebook page.

Step 2: Complete the *Timeline* chart. Cut out the chart. Apply glue to the back and attach it below the title.

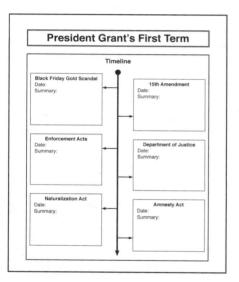

Demonstrate and Reflect on What You Have Learned

Jay Gould and James Fisk were considered "robber barons." Research the term using the Internet or other reference sources. In your interactive notebook, define *robber baron* and list the names of four other famous robber barons.

Robber Barons Jay Gould (left) and James Fisk (right) tried to take over the gold market in 1869.

Key Details

President Grant's First Term

Ulysses S. Grant became the 18th president of the United States on March 4, 1869. He was president over much of the Reconstruction Era. Grant inherited many problems. Northern Republicans and Southern Democrats were still bitter rivals. Each wanted to control the rebuilding of the South.

Grant's lack of political experience soon became apparent. Most **civil service jobs**, or government jobs, were by appointment—from Cabinet members to postmasters in small towns. Grant appointed many personal and army friends to these important jobs. Many of these people also lacked political experience and skills for the positions they received. Grant was often criticized for his poor judgment.

Successes of the Grant Administration

President Grant wanted to restore the Union, protect the civil rights of African Americans, and stop violence and voter intimidation in the South by groups like the Ku Klux Klan (KKK). He worked with the United States Congress to achieve his goals.

- The **Fifteenth Amendment**, which was ratified February 3, 1870, guaranteed the right of all male citizens aged 21 years and older to vote, regardless of race.
- The **Enforcement Acts** were three bills passed between May 31, 1870, and April 20, 1871. They protected African Americans' right to vote, to hold office, to serve on juries, and receive equal protection of laws. The laws authorized Grant to send Federal troops to the South to fight against Southern whites and groups like the KKK who opposed African Americans being able to vote or hold public office.
- The **United States Department of Justice** was established June 22, 1870, with the purpose of cracking down on groups such as the Ku Klux Klan and enforcing Reconstruction and African Americans' civil rights.
- The **Naturalization Act** was passed on July 14, 1870. It allowed persons of African descent to become American citizens.
- On July 15, 1870, Georgia became the last former Confederate state to be readmitted to the Union. During his first term, all former Confederate states were readmitted to the Union.
- The **Amnesty Act** was passed on May 22, 1872. It ended office-holding disqualifications against most of the Confederate leaders and other former civil and military officials who had rebelled against the Union in the Civil War.

Scandals

One of the most disastrous events of Grant's first term was the **Black Friday Gold Scandal**. Two stock investors, Jay Gould and his partner James Fisk, tried to take over the gold market by buying up gold to drive up the price. On September 24, 1869, when Grant realized what they were doing, he ordered $4 million in federal gold sold. That immediately lowered the price of gold and ruined Fisk and Gould's scheme, but it also caused financial ruin for many honest gold investors. It badly affected the economy for several years afterward.

President Grant's First Term

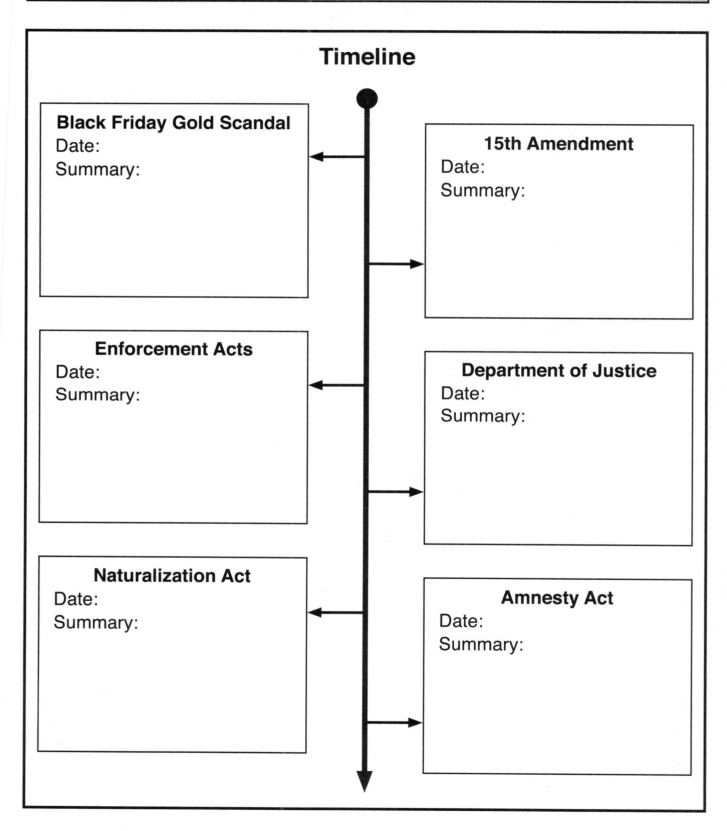

Timeline

Black Friday Gold Scandal
Date:
Summary:

15th Amendment
Date:
Summary:

Enforcement Acts
Date:
Summary:

Department of Justice
Date:
Summary:

Naturalization Act
Date:
Summary:

Amnesty Act
Date:
Summary:

Student Instructions: The Fifteenth Amendment

Materials Needed

Glue, scissors, colored pencils

How to Create a Right-hand Interactive Notebook Page

Read the Key Details page. Then cut out the page and attach it to the right-hand page of your interactive notebook. Use what you have learned to create the left-hand page.

How to Create a Left-hand Interactive Notebook Page

Complete the following steps to create the left-hand page of your interactive notebook. Use lots of color.

Step 1: Cut out the title and glue it to the top of the notebook page.

Step 2: Fill in the blanks on the *15th Amendment* piece. Cut out the piece. Apply glue to the back and attach it below the title.

Step 3: Complete the three *Definition* puzzle pieces. Cut out the pieces. Apply glue to the back of each piece and attach them at the bottom of the page.

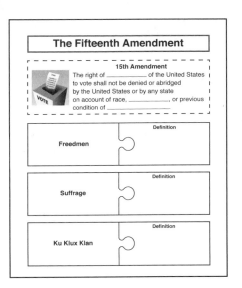

Demonstrate and Reflect on What You Have Learned

Amendments to the United States Constitution become law only when ratified by a specific number of states. On February 3, 1870, the Fifteenth Amendment was approved by 28 states, the required number at the time. Use the Internet or other reference sources to research the processes for amending the Constitution. Today, how many states must approve an amendment before it can be added to the Constitution? Write the answer in your interactive notebook. Support your answer with specific details or examples.

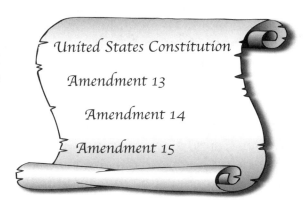

Key Details

The Fifteenth Amendment

The Fifteenth Amendment was one of three Reconstruction Era changes made to the United States Constitution. The **Thirteenth Amendment** abolished slavery in the United States. The **Fourteenth Amendment** granted citizenship and equal rights to men born in the United States, including African-American men. The **Fifteenth Amendment** guaranteed all American citizens (only men aged 21 and over), including formerly enslaved African-American men, the right to vote.

African-American men voting as depicted on the cover of **Harper's Weekly**

Right to Vote

Although the Fourteenth Amendment gave African-American men all rights of citizenship, many were denied those rights, particularly the right to vote. Congress felt it was necessary to add another amendment that very specifically stated that all citizens had the right to vote and that no state could deny that right.

The Fifteenth Amendment was approved by Congress in the last days of President Andrew Johnson's administration. President Grant supported the amendment and worked to get it approved by the states. It was **ratified**, or approved, on February 3, 1870, by 28 states, the required number at the time.

15th Amendment

Section 1. The right of citizens of the United States to vote shall not be denied or abridged by the United States or by any state on account of race, color, or previous condition of servitude.

Opposition to the Fifteenth Amendment

Many in the South refused to accept the rights guaranteed to **freedmen**, formerly enslaved men, by the Fourteenth and Fifteenth Amendments. They denied that freedmen were citizens and denied **suffrage**, or the right to vote, to African-American men. They instead ignored the amendments and continued to prevent freedmen from exercising their political rights to vote or to hold a state or local elected office in the government. In many Southern states, such as Louisiana and Georgia, African-American men were illegally kept from voting by local officials. Violent groups of racist white Southerners like the **Ku Klux Klan**, **intimidated**, or frightened, many African-American men to keep them away from the polls and voting.

Grant Enforces Fifteenth Amendment

President Grant was determined to enforce the Fifteenth Amendment and to protect the civil rights of African Americans. He sent federal troops to Louisiana, Mississippi, and South Carolina to **suppress violence**, or keep violence from happening, against African Americans. He used the newly created Justice Department to enforce the laws, and thousands of Southerners were prosecuted.

The Fifteenth Amendment

15th Amendment

The right of _____ of the United States
to vote shall not be denied or abridged
by the United States or by any state
on account of race, _____, or previous
condition of _____.

Freedmen	Definition

Suffrage	Definition

Ku Klux Klan	Definition

Student Instructions: President Grant's Second Term

Materials Needed

Glue, scissors, colored pencils

How to Create a Right-hand Interactive Notebook Page

Read the Key Details page. Then cut out the page and attach it to the right-hand page of your interactive notebook. Use what you have learned to create the left-hand page.

How to Create a Left-hand Interactive Notebook Page

Complete the following steps to create the left-hand page of your interactive notebook. Use lots of color.

Step 1: Cut out the title and glue it to the top of the notebook page.

Step 2: Cut out the *Election of 1872* flap book. Cut on the solid lines to create three flaps. Apply glue to the back of the gray tab and attach it below the title. Under each flap, write the name of the political party that nominated the candidate.

Step 3: Cut out the *Grant's Administration* flap book. Cut on the solid lines to create four flaps. Apply glue to the back of the gray tab and attach it at the bottom of the page. Under each flap, describe the event.

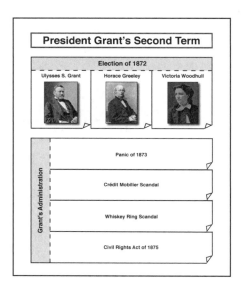

Demonstrate and Reflect on What You Have Learned

Ulysses S. Grant's presidency occurred during a time in history when the government was plagued with corruption. The Pendleton Civil Service Reform Act of 1883 was signed into law by President Chester A. Arthur. Use the Internet or other reference sources to research the law. What was the purpose of the law? Write the answer in your interactive notebook. Support your answer with specific details or examples.

Key Details

President Grant's Second Term

Near the end of Ulysses S. Grant's first term as president, several important members of Congress were mixed up in a scandal involving stolen funds from the Transcontinental Railroad. Grant's vice president, Schuyler Colfax, and other government officials were accused of taking bribes. Grant was not accused of any wrongdoing in the affair, and he remained popular.

Election of 1872

In 1872, Grant was again nominated for president on the first ballot at the national **Republican Party** convention. His new running mate was Senator Henry Wilson of Massachusetts. Republicans concerned with the corruption of the Grant administration formed the **Liberal Republican Party** and nominated Horace Greeley for president and Benjamin Gratz Brown for vice president. The main part of the **Democratic Party** also supported Greeley and Brown. The **Equal Rights Party** nominated the first female for president, Victoria Woodhull. Her running mate was Frederick Douglass, the man who had escaped slavery and become a widely known abolitionist speaker.

Grant remained at the family home during the campaign. At that time, it was unusual for a candidate to campaign for himself. Speeches were given by others but not by the candidates themselves. Grant won the popular vote by an overwhelming majority and received 286 electoral votes. Greeley died before the electoral votes were cast so the electors pledged to him voted for Brown or other Democratic candidates. Woodhull received no electoral votes.

Problems Plagued Grant's Administration

During Grant's second term as president, problem after problem plagued his administration. A severe drop in stock prices caused the financial **Panic of 1873**. Many banks failed and factories closed. The country faced a major economic depression.

Scandals continued to be exposed during Grant's second term in office. The **Crédit Mobilier** scandal of 1872–1873 damaged the careers of several congressmen. The Union Pacific Railroad Company was contracted with building a portion of the Transcontinental Railroad. The company leaders created the Crédit Mobilier of America construction company. They sold or gave shares in this company to influential congressmen. The **Whiskey Ring** scandal in 1875 involved officials of the Treasury Department responsible for collecting taxes on liquor failing to turn over some of the money they collected.

Reconstruction Success

Grant did help the country survive the Reconstruction Era. During his second term, Grant worked with Congress to protect the civil rights of all citizens. On March 1, 1875, Congress passed the **Civil Rights Act**. The law banned **racial discrimination**, or treating someone unfavorably because of race or color. It guaranteed access to things such as public transportation for everyone.

Life After Politics

After retiring from politics, Grant wrote the *Personal Memoirs of U. S. Grant*, a two-volume set about his life. It was a success, earning his bankrupt family thousands of dollars. Grant died of cancer on July 23, 1885, shortly after finishing the memoir.

President Grant's Second Term

Election of 1872

| Ulysses S. Grant | Horace Greeley | Victoria Woodhull |

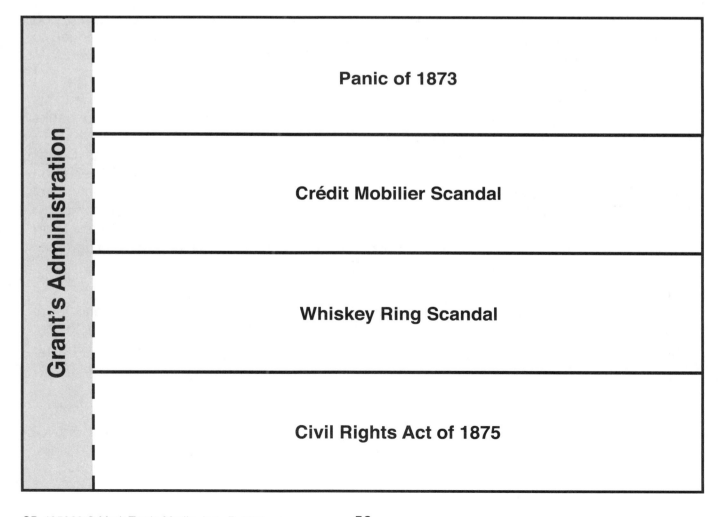

Grant's Administration

Panic of 1873

Crédit Mobilier Scandal

Whiskey Ring Scandal

Civil Rights Act of 1875

Student Instructions: President Rutherford B. Hayes

Materials Needed

Glue, scissors, colored pencils

How to Create a Right-hand Interactive Notebook Page

Read the Key Details page. Then cut out the page and attach it to the right-hand page of your interactive notebook. Use what you have learned to create the left-hand page.

How to Create a Left-hand Interactive Notebook Page

Complete the following steps to create the left-hand page of your interactive notebook. Use lots of color.

Step 1: Cut out the title and glue it to the top of the notebook page.

Step 2: Cut out the *End of the Reconstruction Era* flap book. Cut along the solid lines to create four flaps. Apply glue to the back of the gray center section and attach it below the title.

Step 3: Under each flap, explain the event.

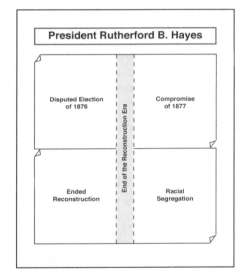

Demonstrate and Reflect on What You Have Learned

Rutherford B. Hayes became the nineteenth president of the United States in 1877. Use the Internet or other reference sources to research the president. How did Hayes earn the nickname "Old Granny?" In your interactive notebook, write the answer. Support your answer with specific details or examples.

Rutherford B. Hayes was declared president by an electoral commission after a disputed election.

Key Details

President Rutherford B. Hayes

Rutherford B. Hayes was a war hero, having risen to the rank of general and having been wounded in the Civil War. Hayes was not associated with any of the corruption of the Grant administration.

Political pins from the 1876 presidential campaign

The Disputed Election of 1876

In the election of 1876, President Grant decided not to run for a third term. At that time, there was no restriction on the number of terms a person could be elected to the office of president. The Republicans nominated Rutherford B. Hayes. Hayes was known for his honesty. As governor of Ohio, he had worked for civil rights for African Americans. The Democrat candidate was Samuel Tilden, governor of New York. He also had a reputation for honesty.

The election was close. When the votes were counted, Tilden had received 250,000 more votes than Hayes. Presidential elections are not based on **popular vote**, however. The deciding factor is the number of **electoral votes** each candidate receives. Each state has a specific number of electoral votes based on its population. To win the election, one candidate must have a majority of the electoral votes.

The Democrats claimed that votes from three Southern states (South Carolina, Florida, and Louisiana) had been falsely counted, and Tilden should have received those electoral votes. Congress set up an **electoral commission** to settle the matter.

Compromise of 1877

As Inauguration Day approached, the election was still in dispute. Finally, an unwritten agreement known as the **Compromise of 1877** was reached. The Democrats agreed not to block Hayes from becoming president if Hayes agreed to withdraw the remaining troops from the South, name a Southerner to his **Cabinet**, or advisory group, and approve federal funds to rebuild the South. As part of the deal, the Democrats promised to protect the civil and political rights of African Americans. On March 2, the commission gave the electoral votes of all three disputed states to Hayes, making him the winner 185 to 184.

End of the Reconstruction Era

The Compromise of 1877 ended the Reconstruction era. Once in office, Hayes withdrew federal troops from Southern states, made federal dollars available for rebuilding the South, and appointed Southerners to government positions. However, the Democrats' promises to protect the rights of African Americans were not kept. The Southern states passed laws that barred African Americans from voting and enforced **racial segregation**, or separation between white people and Black people in public places.

Life After Politics

Hayes refused renomination by the Republican Party in 1880. He died of a heart attack on January 17, 1893.

President Rutherford B. Hayes

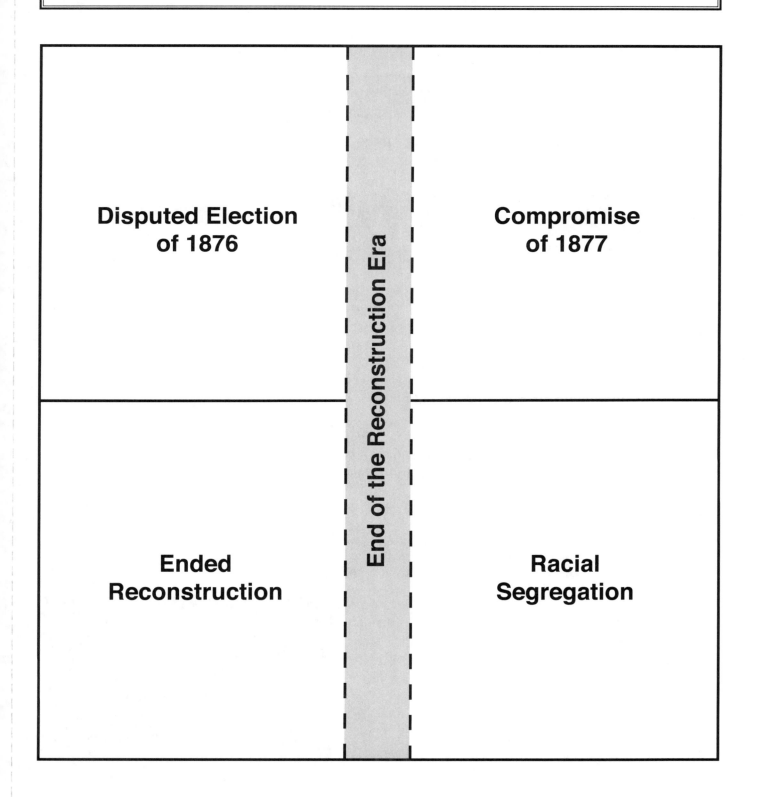

Disputed Election
of 1876

End of the Reconstruction Era

Compromise
of 1877

Ended
Reconstruction

Racial
Segregation

Student Instructions: Jim Crow Laws

Materials Needed

Glue, scissors, colored pencils

How to Create a Right-hand Interactive Notebook Page

Read the Key Details page. Then cut out the page and attach it to the right-hand page of your interactive notebook. Use what you have learned to create the left-hand page.

How to Create a Left-hand Interactive Notebook Page

Complete the following steps to create the left-hand page of your interactive notebook. Use lots of color.

Step 1: Cut out the title and glue it to the top of the notebook page.

Step 2: Complete the *Jim Crow Laws* puzzle piece. Cut out the piece and attach it below the title.

Step 3: Complete the *Definitions* puzzle piece. Cut out the piece and attach it at the bottom of the page.

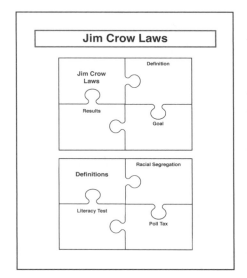

Demonstrate and Reflect on What You Have Learned

The Civil Rights Act of 1964 was signed into law by President Lyndon Johnson. Use the Internet or other reference sources to research the Civil Rights Act of 1964. In your interactive notebook, explain the law. Support your answer with specific details or examples.

President Lyndon Johnson signing the Civil Rights Act of 1964

Jim Crow Laws

"**Jim Crow**" was a character popularized by the white actor Thomas Rice for a **minstrel show**, or song-and-dance routine, in which he impersonated a slave. After the song came out, the term "Jim Crow" became an offensive term often used to refer to African Americans. Soon after, laws directed at African Americans became known as "Jim Crow laws."

Jim Crow Laws

While the federal government controlled the Southern states during Reconstruction, Congress passed the **Civil Rights Act of 1875**, which granted equal rights to African Americans in public accommodations. It made discrimination based on race or color illegal in theaters, hotels, and on railroads and gave African Americans the right to serve on juries. However, during President Hayes' term in office, the Reconstruction Era ended. Southern states once again took control of their governments and began passing **Jim Crow laws** based on race. The goal was to separate the races and to achieve white **supremacy**, or power, over African Americans.

Jim Crow laws required **racial segregation**, or the separation of white people and "persons of color" in **public transportation**, such as streetcars and railroad coaches, and in waiting rooms. Then African Americans were barred from using white barbershops, theaters, and restaurants. Separate schools and state hospitals were built for African Americans. This was a slow process, and it happened at faster or slower paces in different states.

For African Americans who openly opposed the changes, there were segregated prisons and chain gangs. African Americans lived in fear of violent white racists and worried that they were soon going to be losing their jobs.

The **Supreme Court**, the highest judicial court in the United States, upheld the legality of Jim Crow laws in a case in 1896. The Court stated that segregation was legal if "**separate, but equal**" facilities were provided.

Right to Vote

The Fourteenth Amendment guaranteed that states could not deny any person equal protection under the law. The Fifteenth Amendment allowed African-American men to vote. After Reconstruction, Southern states passed Jim Crow laws to make it difficult for African-American men to vote. Many places required voters to pass a **literacy test**, or knowledge test, to be eligible to vote. Since it had been illegal to educate enslaved people in the South, most adult African Americans could not read or write; therefore, they could not vote. Voters were also required to pay **poll taxes**, usually $1 or $2 collected months before the election. Many African Americans could not afford the poll tax. Sometimes, polling places were moved to locations far away from where African Americans lived.

Jim Crow Laws Declared Illegal

It was not until the **Civil Rights Act of 1964** and the **Voting Rights Act of 1965** that Jim Crow laws were made illegal in the United States. The Twenty-fourth Amendment to the U.S. Constitution was also ratified in 1964 to do away with the poll tax. Jim Crow laws were outlawed, but some practices remain in place that make it more difficult for African Americans and other minorities to exercise their right to vote and participate in government and business.

Jim Crow Laws

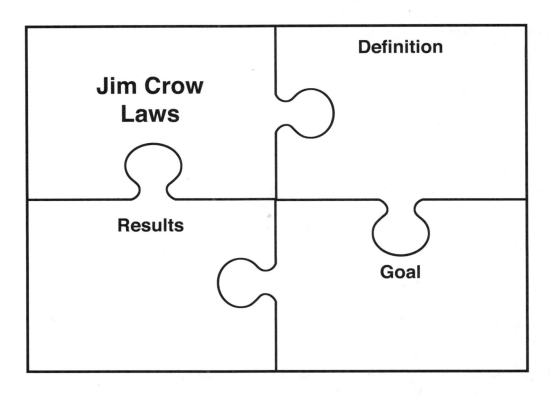

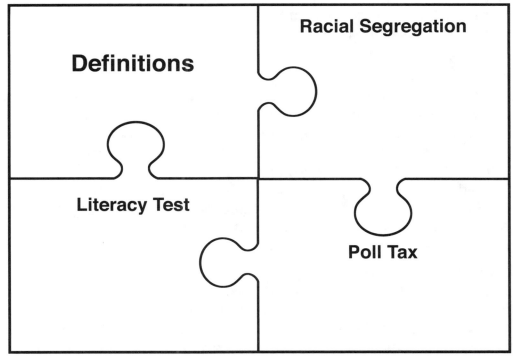